To Ben David :-

Thank you :-

# CUP OF JOY

Enjoy the journey
through the
course in the
Cup of Joy.

*Christopher
Gorgeveni*

# CUP OF JOY

by Christopher Georgeovich

Alive Book Publishing

Cup of Joy
Copyright © 2014 by Christopher Georgeovich

Additional copies may be ordered from the publisher
for educational, business, promotional or premium use.
For information, contact ALIVE Book Publishing at:
alivebookpublishing.com, or call (925) 837-7303.

Book Design by Alex P. Johnson

ISBN-13: 978-1-63132-006-4 Paperback
ISBN-10: 1631320068 Paperback

Library of Congress Control Number: 2014942624

Library of Congress Cataloging-in-Publication Data
is available upon request.

First Edition

Published in the United States of America
by ALIVE Book Publishing and ALIVE Publishing Group,
imprints of Advanced Publishing LLC
3200 A Danville Blvd., Suite 204, Alamo, California 94507
alivebookpublishing.com

PRINTED IN THE UNITED STATES OF AMERICA

10  9  8  7  6  5  4  3  2  1

*Dedicated to the ones I love:*

*My wife Gretchen…*

*who is my true "Cup of Joy!"*

*My brother John…*

*who loves the game more than I do.*

*Jackie and Bill…*

*may their cup runneth over with joy.*

*Liz, who loves tennis.*

*The art of playing golf . . .*
*. . . is not to be played with*

# Introduction

The art of playing golf entails an interplay between men or women and the realm of physics, all on a manicured field. It is filled with emotional, physiological, and physical hazards—and can also be the greatest of fun!

*Fun, that is, when expertise is applied . . .*

Your golf game . . . physics rules you, your club, and your ball. The laws of physics affect the size and weight of the ball, the design of the clubs, and the swing by which the ball is propelled into and across the spaces of air over the fairways and greens.

Each player is a normal person before he or she becomes a golfer.

The ball—well, it was a normal ball before it became a golf ball . . . and the club was just your basic stick, before the stick became a golf club. And the field—merely an open field, before it became a golf course.

The length of each hole varies by the color-coded tee position. Black tees are for professionals. Blue tees are for good golfers who can play the longer distances. White tees are for men beginners, and gold tees are for...not sure! Finally, the red tees are for ladies. The distance, beginning with the tee box and finishing at the green, is the fairway. Along the way, there are trees, the "rough" (a longer grass than that on the fairway), and intentionally placed ponds and bunkers filled with sand—some formidable physical hazards—commonly called sand traps. These, along with objects placed in the way by design, movable or not, such as trees, rocks, hoses, machinery, golf carts and rakes, all, of course, are intended to make the game a little trickier, and more fun.

Except on the "perfect day for golfing," the weather and all of its changes can dominate both emotional and physical hazards simultaneously. The velocity and direction of the wind add elements of excitement to the game. These must be considered with all due respect! Having the right grip on the club, and swinging it properly, will control the ball and send it into the wind with a low trajectory. Controlling the flight will, in most cases, keep the ball on the fairway or land the ball on the green.

That's it! On the green!

In golf, the course topography creates different places where the ball may rest, commonly called lies. Different lies may be situated on a side hill, downhill, uphill, hard pan, underneath shrubs, or next to a tree—all along the expanse of any course. Any one of these will create a mental or physical challenge for golfers focusing on second shots to place the ball on the green.

Climate, too, has effects on the distance the ball will travel on any given day, in any kind of weather. Imagine: On the West Coast during the summer months, with less humidity than in the central states and the East Coast, the ball will travel farther in the drier air. East of the Rockies, the humidity, creating greater resistance on the velocity of the ball, well . . . the distance will be less even when you use the very same club. Physics rules! Because of its closer molecular structure, cold air creates more resistance for the ball's airborne penetration.

# The Learning Curve...
## The Physical and Mental Processes

Let me talk to you . . . yes, you! In golf, all the choices *you* may make are uniquely personal—*your* determinations. When you arrive at the first tee, this becomes clear. Addressing the ball for any shot, you need to be aware of certain aspects: commonsense, physical ability, and personal temperament. It is true! All the fun you will have, including the good shots, the bad shots, and any shots in between, begins with the first drive and ends at the last putt on the eighteenth green.

What happens throughout the course is a journey into your personal world of sport—the joy, the frustration, the physiological and emotional gymnastics of the great sport of golf. Some experiences will seem imprinted into your consciousness forever. In your travels on the course, your guides are your intelligence, experience, and intuition. All that you feel and see before you can have an impact on your decisions. Tapping into these constant guides to support you is essential.

With your mind occupied at any given moment with simply enjoying the experience of playing golf, you may rarely have time to think out the solution for any specific shot at hand. Your playing experience will dictate your shot's execution. This experience will be carried with you until the next time you place a tee in the ground.

After your round, many memories will be reviewed, enjoyed, even revisited many times over. In time, a library of memories is created, ever available in developing your ability to play well. Expertise is a cumulative process, clearly . . . and *the better you play, the more fun you will have, and the more fun you have, the better you will play.* Your memories become your teacher and disciplinarian. As passion bubbles up from the subconscious, its essence will drive you continuously to become efficient at seeing what is not there—the invisible factors—as much as the obvious surroundings, and sometimes a mystical process ensues. Your subconscious continues molding you into a better player—aha! Even without your permission! And this is how the inner game is played and the player in the game of golf evolves.

Certain aspects of the game become apparent through familiarizing yourself with the clubs in relation to striking the ball and moving it forward. These new discoveries will expose you to an "aha" moment! These "aha" moments are the catalyst that cement the physical action to the mental processes in playing golf. As these emotional and thoughtful insights grasping your curiosity to further develop your abilities, a new thinking will interrupt your consciousness. You are now in " Never Never Land." You will never be the same, and you will never be normal ever again. When this chemistry is in motion your golfing addition will change your life, if you so choose. It's your personal decision. That is, if you are able to deny yourself this involvement in having such a relationship with the game.

*By definition, by its very nature, in fact, mediocre golf needs improvement.* This is clearly often upsetting to players who respect the game. Taking responsibility to learn all aspects of playing properly is actually an opportunity. Since it is a social game, having proper etiquette and behaving appropriately are as important and necessary as playing well. Moreover, golf in its extensive dynamic is an international sport that enhances social and commercial relations around the world. Friendships are created that can last a lifetime, all because one plays the game of golf well.

## The Zone

After an excellent level or standard of play has been reached, a quiet serenity will take hold and carry you throughout the course This sensation is commonly called concentration or a sense of being "in the zone." In this state of altered consciousness, magic happens; a communion of joy infuses your actions. Nothing much else matters except your sense of harmony . . . your club, your ball, and a fairway that supports you in playing—not to mention the camaraderie of your foursome or fellow players along the way.

As your ability to play better golf increases, you become aware that golf is a discipline and must be played with thoughtfulness so as not to disturb others and yourself. Synergy will carry you on. Your consciousness will assist you in choosing the proper club for the needed distance to reach each unique objective. It will also help create confidence in your swing. Watching the trajectory of a ball is exciting, awesome, exhilarating—yet sometimes even disturbing. Controlling the trajectory on a windy day will benefit your scoring greatly—should the wind simply take off with your ball, however, your inner peace might be temporarily rattled! Not one golfer has escaped effects like these; these tactical challenges await each player on the tee.

By contrast, making a precise shot to a specific location on the fairway or green is a joy (not to mention that your group applauds your success) and you all feel completely exhilarated.

Knowing what a ball's trajectory will do when the ball is accurately struck will increase your appreciation and confidence. Your consciousness awakens to the reality that to play well you need to be completely mentally alert. As consciousness possesses wisdom beyond simply the rational state of being, allowing the more holistic dynamics and environment to work for you is one of many keys to finding the fun side of expert golfing.

In developing your internal game, direct the biomechanics toward greater efficiency. Within those moments when it works right, you experience some universal magic. You will not realize how often this magic occurs until you feel it, and believe it exists. Courage needed for difficult shots will rise to the surface, while your mind erases hesitations against completing even risky golfing actions—and so the art of playing golf comes to life. It may take time to grasp the magical aspects and the naturalness of this amazing mystical quality.

After this level has been experienced, an elusive invisible door opens quietly within your mind, and your mind's ear begins to perceive a sound. The hum is so soft that at times you cannot even hear it. Only when you begin to listen will the sound be heard. A faint exciting vibration will play upon your heartstrings. You will begin to walk on a softer grass. Your consciousness has awakened. Your whole body, mind, and soul will begin the play. You are inside the art of the play itself!

In my case, this sensation always comes with a sense of being given a gift.

This vibration has the same primary source of energy as the life force that daily flows through you. It stays hidden and dormant until awakened by your desire to play the game seriously. Then your awakened consciousness will deliver the sense of synchronicity and harmony of the varied aspects of the *whole* play and game. Holistically, you are in the mystical zone, absorbed into complete participation, totally possessed by the magic of this awareness—with joy as the reward. Your game is now on cruise control. Your altered state of consciousness begins directing your every decision with much greater ease.

## My Dad and I

I've felt a desire to play at Pebble Beach that reaches back in my memory to 1968, when my dad and I walked its elegant beauty together. We were having a wonderful time enjoying each other's company among thousands of spectators in the gallery. Most of time was spent walking the nearby Cypress Point golf course, which was on the circuit of courses to play in the "Crosby Clambake" tournaments of that time.

Several yards just in front of us, we saw . . . guess who!

Bing Crosby was striding toward the Cypress Point clubhouse. In the 1930s, my dad, when in his teens, had spoken with Bing while the latter was making a road film at Pine Studios, in London. This time, as Crosby walked in the front door of the private clubhouse, we missed the opportunity for my dad to say hello. We were disappointed but felt better after visiting the concession stand and walking around Cypress.

This was for sure the most elegant piece of real estate on which I have ever walked. Deer casually grazing among the sculpted, windblown cypresses were receiving more attention than the golfers. And the people in the gallery were equally entertaining for the deer

My dad and I also walked the fairways at Pebble, viewing the manicured greens of golf, those greens having been dignified by all the greats in golf history. These experiences are treasured parts of my memories. Celebrities of Hollywood and American industry have played with the golf professionals in the "Crosby Clambake." Ever since 1919, the Pebble Beach course has hosted dignitaries, luminaries, and lovers of the art of the game. Many have experienced this same love of the game— not just a hobby, not just a sport . . . but the art that it truly is.

A green canvas painted with frustration, happiness, and joyful tears of triumph, as well as exhilarating life lessons all around.

## A Game of Love:
## Adventures at Pebble Beach

Ideas arrive unexpectedly.

They can come at unexpected times and quite often need to be quickly grasped, even written down, so as not to escape into the atmosphere whence they came. The idea came to me during Thanksgiving 1999 to play the Pebble Beach Golf Links in California on my sixtieth birthday. After learning and playing golf for several years only on public courses, I desperately wanted to play on a Class A course. A dream come true was about to happen . . . close friends, golf lovers like me, were invited to celebrate my sixtieth birthday week-end at Pebble Beach—and together we would once again find the art of golf's synergistic surprises all part of the fun!

I created an invitation with the date, time, lodging, and tee time at Pebble Beach. Presenting the invitation to my brother John during Christmas week caught him totally by surprise. He didn't believe me, but finally became convinced. On Christmas Eve, I gave the invitation to Bill and his wife, Jackie. Bill was stunned with disbelief. To my surprise, Jackie became quite emotional and had to call her father in Oregon. She was overwhelmed with tears of joy. The delight she was expressing gave me such pleasure. I think I felt better than she did.

In life, giving has a greater personal merit than receiving your favorite desire. To play inside the ropes at Pebble was a dream we'd never expected to come true. It started in motion as a possibility, and then became a most wonderful reality. When pursued, a little idea can change dreams into reality.

In my humble opinion, life is about dreaming, doing, and sharing.

Pebble Beach possesses aspects of amazing magic and mystique. On the physical level alone, it is probably the most elegant and beautiful course in the entire world. The venue itself inspires a shining sense of reverence. It is a divinely designed creation, expressing charm and a design both truly strong and graceful. For devoted golfers, it is a glimpse of heaven, especially on a bright and sunny California day. Those who have chipped out of the rough, or out of the bunkers, and those who have taken pleasure in putting the delightful small greens—all have shared the real joys of the game on perhaps the best course in the world.

On a normal day, the player feels fragrant sea air gently blowing onto the fairways, hears graceful, frothy waves dancing on the shores in the distance, and basks in the sparkling sunshine on this warm and welcoming course.

Large galleries with dedicated fans fill the tournament events—including my wife and me. Gretchen and I walked outside the ropes for more than twenty years, watching the best of the best with joy in our hearts. Those memories are priceless. And this very same course has created memories for hundreds of thousands of people worldwide, more experiences never to be forgotten.

For me, Pebble carries reasons for respect in every blade of grass, every grain of sand, and in every leaf on the trees. For those lucky enough to play the course, walking on the fairways inside the ropes feels like being inside a place of worship, paying deep respects. No matter what the weather, the golf course at Pebble Beach exudes dignity from every point, and every point of view.

Oddly enough, as I was driving to the course from the San Francisco area that Sunday morning, January 23, 2000, what was on my mind was golf wear! How's that? Yes! Our "golf wear"! For several weeks I'd been weighing what to wear on that course, where class, style, taste, and fit are of the utmost concern. Looking good is paramount on most private courses, but the one where we were about to play, well . . . it was absolutely essential to the art! After all, this was the great Pebble Beach, where historically famous players had touched down, performing miracles in front of hundreds of thousands in the golfing galleries, all watching these amazing professionals — Jack Nicklaus, Tiger Woods, and many, many others.

My mind was totally out to lunch with excitement just because I was about to play the famous course. I didn't think of buying a rain suit and did have rain gear in my bag, but it was all too old and tasteless for this special occasion. And as it turned out, the weather was so horrible that my well-worn rain gear didn't make a difference. Hard to believe, but simple survival itself came more into question as time went on that day.

Surviving a round of golf in a heavy rainstorm on the central
California Coast is not a foregone conclusion. Dumb people
do have their behavioral problems—that we all know—and
that day we created our own for the sake of having fun. To
put it mildly, we could have been statistics, tragic figures, fa-
talities—headlines, in fact! "Golfers Blown off Cliff into Roiling Surf." "Golfer Slips in Bunker and Drowns in Two Feet
of Rainwater—Man Unable to Keep His Balance in Gale Force
Winds." With this scenario, the press would have had a hey-
day! But guess what! The universe *does* care for even those of
us who become dumb, windblown golfers. My prayer wheel
was constantly in motion and still is, unlike my mind, which
on such occasions takes leave of its senses—goes off on a hike!

A wet day of misery did not actually enhance the chances of
our having the anticipated wonderful time, but this is how
we began the joyous weekend of living our golf-obsessed
dreams. All excited and ready to play, we had traveled some
two hundred miles on a wet, sobering road in the most mis-
erable windy weather. It was my birthday, as I said, and that
sense of fantasy just momentarily started to wane—but then
the waning faded, too! A quiet inner voice kept saying, "Yes!
It's going to happen." I will maintain my golf fantasy until
the end of time! My foursome will get there and enjoy our
day. Happy Birthday to me! Happy Birthday to me! And it
was indeed a happy sixtieth, as it turned out.

The weekend before this one had provided perfect weather
to play golf by the ocean. This one, to put it mildly, was the
worst weather in golf history, or so it seemed. This date was
the only one available to us per the ownership. Arriving the

evening before at Spanish Bay Lodge, we were shown to our accommodations, where we cleaned up, and then trotted off to Roy's for dinner. The excitement started slowly and gently to catch hold. I was delightfully surprised after dinner when my friend Bill asked me to come out onto the patio, where a bagpiper—literally—came out of the mist playing "Happy Birthday" to me. I was completely knocked out by the gesture and a little emotional.

By evening's end we were in a prime emotional state to grip it and rip it. To say the least, I didn't sleep soundly that night before the most anticipated golf date in my life. Why would I sleep? My friends and I were going to play the most beautiful course we had ever played in our lives tomorrow! No one slept soundly.

A steady downpour was continuous throughout the night, a hardly obscure omen left unheeded by us all. With wind velocity up to forty-five miles per hour as we drove over to the course, we had no idea what the wind's behavior would be *on* the course. Of all the days of the year, even all the days of my golfing life, it had to storm on the treasured day I had set aside to play—my rare and one and only sixtieth birthday. You see, this project, to treat my friends to a round of golf, to be inside the ropes on my birthday, had been planned with a lot of forethought. Then to have Mother Nature pull rank with a major downpour was pure treachery. This is what I thought before the experience. But, now, indeed, I think differently.

One of the unbreakable rules of golf is that come rain, wind, or fire, you must be on the first tee on time. Well. *We* were, but the starter had other ideas. The staff at the pro shop had been unsure (weather or not—ha, ha) whether they would even open the course for play at all, so, it was a time of indecision. We had a choice—to give up or to stay and wait to play. Ours was to play. Here there could be no "mutiny," for certain! We were all on board. This decision was based on both time and financial considerations.

To fulfill my dream, decisions had been made for the sake of the interested parties . . . my costs, their time, our health, and experiences. A dream held by all of us for, say, three entire decades was becoming reality. Wow! We were going to play Pebble Beach! But there we were, in the worst weather we had ever experienced! What to do? It would be unthinkable to be here at Pebble, but unable to play. It's also unthinkable, really, in the golfing world that a little rain, with thirty-mile-per-hour wind gusts would deter or indeed even prevent us from playing. Good golfing morning!

So we waited inside an empty coffee shop, eating an anxious breakfast. None of us really tasted our meal as we viewed the first tee from the upstairs vantage point overlooking the practice green. Our dream of playing that morning was vanishing like the downpour into the ground. All that planning and daydreaming about playing on the international golf course was up in the (drenched) air, gone with the wind into a world of regret.

Our thoughts were preoccupied with walking the green fairways of Pebble Beach at last, and the starter delayed things for a very stressful two hours. But before breakfast ended, the first tee was opened. Time to put on the rain gear, people! It's tee time! We had brought our "A" game whether the rain came in buckets or as drizzles. All that nervousness at breakfast seemed to become fuel to play the course under the present conditions.

The starter was well aware of the radical weather conditions as he sent us sloshing out to the first tee. What's more, after the first eight holes, the marshals started to rush our play—badgering us, in fact, which was deeply upsetting to say the least. We had never played the course before. The wind, the rain, the wet fairways, the wet rough—you get the picture, right? Well, the *pros* would never play under those conditions. We, though, were being sent onward, directly into the storm, by the starter, with zip concern for our welfare.

You see, a complete rain check just wasn't available.

After all the years of playing horribly in great weather on city and county courses, now we were playing the most picturesque course in the world, and our experience was rewarded by total saturation in a mini-hurricane! Pebble Beach is a golfing theater that normally bathes in warm sunlight over visual grandeur. On this day the stage was like a ferocious roaring bear. We were being soaked with blistery cold rain with every shot we took.

Despite this unexpected blast of environmental defiance, however, delightful fun arrived unexpectedly in various experiences on the course. Stormy weather provided its own joyful moments as our noses were became numb as we became soaked in the heat of battle.

On that special day at Pebble Beach Golf Links, the wind and rain set the stage for our heightened focus with a highly melodramatic atmosphere. It was the most memorable single round of golf my friends and I have ever had on those wet fairways—never to be forgotten. For this game, and a game of love it was, Mother Nature had set the stage perfectly for us all to have the most fun, the most frustration, the most enjoyable round of golf we will always cherish as friends.

The essential point is that we had to *be there*—completely *involved in our game on all levels*—in order to survive the round. Mother Nature played her part so well during the game, that without her participation our experiences would have been totally conventional, blab and forgotten.

## The First Hole: Par Four, Blue Tee, 376 Yards

Helping us remain focused while we were approaching the first tee was the finest of furiously foul weather! Windswept precipitation came down way too generously, though the first tee remained sheltered somewhat from the wind by a stand of tall trees on the fairway's right side. The treetops were moving wildly, swaying in some gusty winds, warning us of turbulence on the other side.

The first fairway has a dogleg right about 220 yards out, which passes through a narrow opening toward the ocean onto a slightly elevated green. At that point the grandeur of the sweeping Pacific Ocean comes into view.

Who teed off first? I'm not sure. We all had decent spots from which to play the second shot, taking us from a wet fairway into the windy corridor of angry weather coming off the ocean. Bracing against this strong wind brought on a slight sense of anxiety that transformed into a touch of excitement about addressing the shot.

That was just an introduction to the amount of wind and water we were going to encounter for the rest of our play. I didn't reach the green. The wind from the ocean caught the ball and dropped it straight down into the four-inch rough several feet from the green. I chipped onto the saturated green and two-putted through the water-soaked turf.

We all acknowledged, then and there, that we were playing Pebble Beach in the worst conditions we had observed in years of watching the "Crosby Clambakes" and AT&T-sponsored tournaments at the course.

The original "clambake" was played in the first week of January. Because of the risk of foul weather, the tournament was changed to the second week in February after AT&T took over sponsorship. I was so excited about playing Pebble, the foul weather in January had slipped out of my consciousness altogether.

We had a good laugh over the conditions in which we were playing, and then continued to the second tee box.

## The Second Hole: Par Five, Blue Tee, 562 Yards

The second hole, slightly descending toward the unseen green, is completely exposed to all weather elements. The fairway runs south, parallel to the ocean, about five hundred yards from the cliffs, with the cliffs protecting the course from the ocean's continuous wave swells.

At our first view of the roiling Pacific Ocean, *awesome* describes the feeling; and that is one gigantic understatement.

Admiring the ocean and its tremendous power, we realized that unbelievably, we were standing on the second fairway. Finally inside the ropes, we were playing Pebble Beach after all the years we had walked outside the ropes as part of the gallery. Gusts of wind carrying sheets of water across the fairway only slightly aggravated our initial enjoyment.

As I swung left-handed, the wind was coming into my back at thirty or so miles per hour. A rude awakening was what we were in for that day, but the excitement of playing the second hole at Pebble overrode any trivial concerns about the weather. The gale-force winds were of more concern than the rain, in fact. Addressing the shots was difficult. Balance while swinging the club was my main concern. Playing a low driver into the left side of the fairway, just touching the rough, was the thing to do . . . then a three-wood to about a hundred yards from the green. Protected by a cluster of tall trees, the green had a narrow opening to the pin. The third shot landed at the back of a very slow, wet green. A three-putt was in order. Done!

At this point, the water was coming directly into my rain suit. I was getting soaked. Despite the rain, after a one-nanosecond attitude check, we all felt good about playing in the storm. Off we went, to the third tee.

*An Insight*

*There is such a vastness of game knowledge required in the art of golf. Totally necessary is realizing that golf is a contact sport, yet not in the classic sense of the cliché. This is one little-known fact.*

*Contact, in a split second, is made at high speed—at times, the player is not even looking. His or her anticipation is controlling the vision, as the eyes dart forward before contact is executed. But curiosity spoils the shot. Anchoring one's vision behind the ball is the answer in seeing the contact of the club as it is striking the ball. Delicate shots around the green demand that the golfer stare at the back of the ball.*

*Contact at the point of the drive depends on great speed with pinpoint accuracy and delivery with a lighting strike. A good contact is felt within the golfer's whole body, mind, and soul. In all ball sports and in others, sound contact is featured as a major skill in the game. Contact is practiced at a golf range. When that happens with great accuracy, one's being vibrates with gratitude and delight.*

## The Third Hole: Par Four, Blue Tee, 327 Yards

A dogleg left with a wooded ravine hazard on the left side of a medium-wide fairway staring into the wind. Rain was coming in sheets, blown in with the power of a freight train, right off the ocean onto the fairway and where? into our faces. What would we do now? A commitment had been solidified among us at the first tee. Our only choice was to proceed forward with caution through the raindrops and not be blown over on our backsides by the gusts of wind. Would we survive the onslaught of weather with wet smiles, or wet tears? Attitude matters, always above all.

On the tee, we were standing in a diagonal row, Jackie first, Bill second, John third, and yours truly last. All golfers *extra-ordinaire*! All celebrating our love of the game . . . but . . . oops! Jackie addressed her drive, took her normal backswing, and lost her grip and her driver. The club went flying over everyone's head, landing with a loud splat just behind me. I was watching her address her drive and saw her driver fly through the rain with the greatest of ease—in my direction. "Would this be your club, Jackie?"

With that, we all cracked up, and any lingering tensions were broken. We were bound to grip it and rip it, *weather* or not! Fun and enjoyment were on the menu for the rest of the round. So we thought at that moment.

With my adrenaline rising, my drive went over the dogleg into the wet rough, without my realizing how close the dogleg was to the tee. The second shot stayed in the wet four-inch rough about seventy yards out. The third shot dived into the bunker protecting the small, sloped green, a bunker that was already half full with water. The ball was removed with ease, though. Two putts later, I was walking toward the fourth tee box.

We took inventory of one another's condition . . . all good to go on. We were beginning to settle into the existing conditions without distress or complaint. Having found courage in playing the third hole, we survived with delighted smiles across our wet faces, and moved along.

## The Fourth Hole: Par Four, Blue Tee, 327 Yards

A narrow, straight fairway running south along the water's edge, just above a small beach named Pebble. The tee is positioned perpendicular to the seventeenth tee. Both are located close to the swim club by Stillwater Cove. Large groups of the gallery, in professional events, gather at this location. Two greens, the sixteenth and the third, with two tees also located at this intersection along with a concession stand—this area is a Times Square of the Pebble Beach course configuration. At times, nearly three hundred people gather there, casually conversing about everything, moving freely among the crowds, with the coolness of a school of fish . . . courtesy freely expressed. All gathered are happy to be there—on any bright, sunny California day, that is!

A small grove of tall cypress trees creates a passageway into a slight swale in the middle of the fairway, leading up to an elevated oval-shaped green surrounded by large cypress trees, next to a wooded ravine leading to the unseen ocean, below on the right side. Gusting winds blew carelessly across the latter part of the fairway, posing questions about which club to choose off the tee. A low, piercing shot is recommended in this situation. I chose to punch my three fairway wood through the porous rain. Luckily, the ball landed about 170 yards out in the center of the fairway, just below an open-face drainage ditch.

In golf, as in any activity, each first decision leads to the next. The first choice has to be correct to carry the weight of the second one. Golf consists of a constant stream of such thoughtful action.

Golf is about choices and decisions made quickly, almost by nature, so as not to disrupt the game. Your decision is as important as the shot you are about to make . . . like a chess game out in an open meadow, if you will, complete with obstacles all around. Quietude must be maintained in your mind as one of the vital challenges in this amazing, yet natural and enjoyable, discipline.

In this "school of golfing," even the act of simply walking toward your next shot gives a golfer time to free himself or herself from the stress of any previous shot.

With my second shot landing on the slightly elevated green, my confidence grew in the decision I had made to play despite the storm. The club I chose for my second shot into the fourth green was a seven-iron.

Two-putted, making par on the fourth hole. Got it done! What storm?

*Observations on Playing the Game*

*An interesting golf characteristic is its agglomeration of choices and decisions: unspoken and invisible codes or rules directing the player in each round. The player, then, becoming aware of how ethical codes apply in the game, learns more as he or she encounters various situations—and they are innumerable.*

*A shared code of conscious behavior is expressed on the course, also, among the foursome as playing goes on. This bonding is normal on any golf course during a round and discontinued afterward until another round is played.*

*Playing the Shot*

*Each lie places its own demands on the shot—the point where all the fun begins. Choosing the correct club, applying the necessary action and force in contacting the ball, while maintaining attitude in executing the shot—these are all vital elements of addressing each particular shot. One's mind has lapses into forgetfulness, which interferes with the game. This affects the quality of one's play as confidence can wane, not because of an inability, but because of this memory lapsing . . . a major problem. While playing golf, maintaining a high level of concentration is totally necessary for protection against disrupting interference.*

*"Stay cool under pressure" is the mantra as one plays.*

## The Fifth Hole: Par Three, Blue Tee, 187 Yards

Secluded high on a bluff, this par three overlooks the ferocious surf below, a dangerous location in some players' view. Large waves careening onto the enormous boulders protects a narrow beach covered with pebbles. . . . As we played, we could see that the wind and rain were dancing all over the fairways of the next six holes we were about to play. These greens were unprotected. Literally, we were in the elements!

Trees protected my back as I struck a three-wood a couple of yards past the pin. The rain and wind subsided as I putted for my bird; the ball passed a few inches beyond the pin. After my par putt, we walked out into the expansive vista of the southern portion of the vast and elegant Pebble Beach course. Located in the center, the fifth green fully opens up to the picturesque landscape Pebble Beach offers to those who come to play and enjoy. The wonderful, breathtaking views surrounding the Pebble Beach's greens have been seen by growing numbers of golf fans and their families, not to mention thousands upon thousands of golfers . . . as well as the world at large through professional tournament play on television.

Before moving on to the sixth hole, we admired the large, stately homes around, each with such sophisticated landscaping adorning the perimeter of the fourteenth fairway. Appreciating this was like having a field day; I noted every detail, totally captivating my being. I felt as though I were walking through a refined playground inside the pages of *Architectural Digest*. Having the good fortune of being on the green at Pebble Beach overwhelmed me. All those years of standing in the gallery had only increased my personal respect and appreciation for this beautiful place.

## The Sixth Hole: Par Five, Blue Tee, 500 Yards

A monster!

This hole has to be with handled with total concentration! The sixth has a fairway demanding every ounce of human respect. An elevated green atop a small mountain covered with heavy rough. The designer must have been a genius! You see? The drive has to be left-center of the fairway, and any shot along the right side is in danger of going down the steep bank into the rough or the ocean. Not to mention the wind gusts that day . . .

My drive, against the wind, ended up in the low, shallow center fairway. It took a good three-wood to get to the bottom of the small mountain supporting the elevated green. The wind was having a fun time blowing rain into my face. The degree of the grade going up the mountain had to be navigated by my third shot to the green. It did land in the left rough next to the green. The wind was howling in my ears while the third putt dropped into the cup. A bogie was a wonderful conclusion to playing the windy, wet monster of a sixth hole.

The view from the sixth green is grand, with a vista that needs to be personally experienced to be appreciated.

## The Seventh Hole: Par Three, Blue Tee, 116 Yards

For several years, my best friend Gretchen, who is also my wife, and I used to picnic by the seventh tee. Spreading a small blanket and sitting on canvas chairs, we would sip wine and munch on some peanut butter sandwiches, fruit, and candy. We greeted the players and gallery as the participants all passed by our picnic location. At times, Gretchen would read or nap while I enjoyed a walk around. Those memories are filled with laughter and great conversational snippets; the gallery of memories is forever treasured and on occasion surfaces to my surprised delight.

One of the *scariest* holes on the course, the seventh will bring anyone to their knees to pray! This hole lies up on a promontory extending several yards out over the Pacific surf. It felt like a window flying open as I stepped up to the tee, the wind rushing into my face, the spot receiving all the turbulent weather that was coming all the way from the Hawaiian Islands. *Pacific* was *not* an accurate description upon arriving at this oceanside seventh hole.

With the flag fluttering at maximum speed, the 116-yard seventh was laughing and talking to me. "I've been waiting for you. Choose your club, Christopher." (Any club, but it must be *the perfect* one!) I chose to punch a six-iron for control, with a low trajectory into the thirty-five-mile-per-hour winds. The ball responded better than anticipated, landing on the green in front and rolling past the pin to the back of the green.

To this day, it is hard to believe I parred the seventh in that storm at Pebble. I give thanks to those deities in charge of my success at that hole. It is known all over the golfing world that this short fairway deserves even the respect of the golfing superstars, and I do regard it with my sincerest sense of respect.

## The Eighth Hole: Par Four, Blue Tee, 416 Yards

While we were standing on the eighth tee, backsides to the storm, the course marshal showed up. We introduced ourselves, chatting about the weather, and he shared some instruction on playing the eighth hole. With winds behind, I was hoping to let the shaft out. To my great surprise, it happened.

My second shot was lying about fifty yards away from the edge of the (very scary) cliff. The remaining fairway is a gaping gorge, about two hundred yards wide.

Over my years as a spectator, seeing the professionals make that shot onto the postage-size green on the edge of the opposing cliff was no less than miraculous. Never in my wildest dreams could I picture my own shot addressing that lie, over that gaping gorge glazed over with salted ocean air. But now it was real. As the green was so very close to the edge of the cliff, the marshal mentioned that I should play the shot to the left about fifty yards. With the wind again at my back I wanted to go for the green. The saturated wind was working with me, so I aimed the shot about twenty yards to the left.

The perfect shot found the kidney-shaped, sloppy trap. The ball landed pin-high in the soaked bunker. Two sloppy mud shots and two wet putts ended the wet and windy adventure across the respected gorge protecting the eighth green. In my opinion, with all of its drama, my ball crossing the gorge was a study in experiencing fear with a touch of arrogance. To make such a commitment needed all that fear and arrogance could bring forth! It instilled in me valuable confidence that carried through the rest of the course.

## The Ninth Hole: Par Four, Blue Tee, 416 Yards

The ninth tee was the beginning of a whole 'nother adventure!

A different marshal came by in a cart and started to speak to John, my brother. After a short conversation, John was very upset. No one was behind us, but this marshal told my brother to speed up play. We were all perturbed at hearing what was said. The game that day was costing us more than two thousand dollars, on this very special course, and yet we were being told to rush the play. For whatever reason, the marshal decided to tail us along the way. So clearly, staying *on purpose* was under siege. Keeping our minds quiet in the stormy weather and maintaining control in the game would be difficult enough for all of us. And John gets very upset when his concentration is disturbed when he's playing golf. Like a rabid dog, to describe this feeling, he in turn upsets me. In this case, our game took a leave. Everyone seemed to become infected with negative energy. Not a good thing!

Running parallel to the beach, the straight fairway on the ninth hole gradually descends to the green, and it had us heading into some forceful wind and rain. With our minds irritated, well . . . we had ten holes yet to play. The irritability was beginning to dampen the joy of the game.

Playing the ninth hole was on the verge of boring. The excitement had been erased by the mental disturbance, so I had to work to dislodge the negative thoughts while walking the wet fairway. As they gradually quieted again, the ninth once again became enjoyable—all systems go, and back on purpose. A bogie was a good conclusion to the ninth. Just call me the "bogie man!"

## The Tenth Hole: Par Four, Blue Tee, 462 Yards

With a flat fairway heading obliquely toward Carmel Beach, again we were confronted by piercing winds and rain. The shots on the tenth fairway remain a blank to me. Maybe it was a double bogie on this one, if memory serves. Remnants of the prior disturbance were still vibrating slightly in my body. Frustration and feeling cold in the windy, damp air definitely prevented better play. Playing golf in this weather is strictly a challenge—when dealing with both Mother Nature and a frustrated consciousness.

But the place drew us back into its pleasures! An extra delight and sense of treasure on the Pebble Beach course was seeing the white stone French-style chateau overlooking the sands of Carmel Beach. Not a single soul was walking on this pristine white beach, normally a real attraction with people drawn to it just like bees to honey. People play in the warm damp sand and walk along the foaming surf with their families—on nice, sunny summer days.

Now a totally mystical view lay before me consisting of the roaring surf, the wind and rain moving through the branches of the leaning cypress trees . . . all of this was without comparison in its beauty around the glistening chateau.

Being in the center of this vortex of beauty was awesome—as was the gaining of a sense of expertise through dramatic perseverance, and a growing faith in my ability to play out such a stormy game of golf—nothing *mini* about it—with my good friends.

*An Observation*

*Playing in a threatening storm is a game very different from playing in any other weather condition. On the fairways, soggy and heavy with water, taking a divot is not advisable for the average golfer. The air is saturated with cold water, the mind in an altered state of consciousness. Yet concentration has to zero-in on the shot at hand. At the same time, the physical body is trying to stay calm and warm. Even standing still is a challenge. You cannot allow your mind to stray from its objective and play golf as if it were bright and sunny outside.*

*All the elements are aligned against a belief in your chances of success. This challenge is for you and your determination, your mental gymnastics and tenacious determination to play golf in a storm. All the decisions made from the start on out hinge on your decision to play, or not to play. And more than halfway through, there is little question about the choice you made!*

*Whatever happens on the course will have to be fun. You are inside a washing machine cycle that will not stop at your command. Your reward must be the experience received by your positive decision to play on through the storm. You must make the best of it by changing perspective, attitude, and perception. Scoring is not the main objective when playing in the rain; it's the expert executing of shots in the wind and pouring rain.*

*An examination of your personal ability to play golf in a storm will create a credit in your personal integrity account. Decisions are at times character builders, which also create future bragging rights, or memories for filling up interesting albums to recall events down the road. Quitting does not enter the equation.*

*At times, commonsense and decision-making do not walk hand in hand. They are so far removed from each other that it's hard to believe it was the same mind that made the choice. Passion is the driving force, where a great deal of time and experience had been invested in learning about the art of golf, experientially. The desire to play the game in any weather conditions is the reason you are here on the tee.*

*So be happy! Don't worry! Just swing!*

## Heading Home
## The Eleventh Hole: Par Four, Blue Tee, 430 Yards

With our backs to the wind, the relatively benign eleventh tee became a ferocious tunnel of concern. My stability when addressing the ball was more like a rock 'n' roll dance. The swing faltered; the drive expected to fly forever just didn't, and instead landed in the gaping bunker on the left side of the fairway. At times, well, bad things happen to good players! Best not to presume any outcomes in advance. This held true with my drive.

Hey! It felt like some of the pieces of my mind were scattered all over this Pebble Beach course! I had no choice but to gather the fractured pieces back together.

In the bunker, I chose a seven-iron to get out. There was enough room beneath the protruding lip to take a good swing. The resulting precarious shot landed into the rough about thirty feet from the front-sloping green. A pitch to the pin, and two putts later, I humbly walked off the green.

The physical setting for this eleventh green is dramatic. There is an estate above the pin, regal and substantial, with what must be a broad, panoramic view of Carmel Beach and Point Lobos. Awesome views, once again! But even the glamorous setting around the green could add little joy to "putting out" and completing the 11th hole. Folks watching the storm from inside the mansion would be more comfortable than any of us out here putting on the wet green. These bits and pieces of inquiring thoughts, well . . . I will gather them up for posterity on some other, sunny day instead.

## The Twelfth Hole: Par Three, Blue Tee, 201 Yards

Unlike the eleventh fairway corridor, the twelfth's sloping fairway is sheltered by a wall under some brush and trees. Looking toward the twelfth green, we could see the course marshal again, sitting in a cart observing us. It was agitating to see this silent observer as we walked up to the tee.

My tee shot dribbled off the tee as the marshal's presence intruded into my head, even altering my swing. All of my eight lies were chunked on the slippery fairway. The marshal continued watching as I walked off the green. My muddied consciousness and I limped toward the next tee for some relief. I did not allow the invasive observer to tap a rowdy two-step on my mind. And ignoring him worked—the marshal drove off into the storm.

Trying to restore harmony to my thoughts while anger and resentment at the deficiencies of course management were pounding away within, I fought back with every ounce of experience. Calming my mind as quickly as possible was paramount. All golfers are blessed with the grace of forgetfulness to help them survive the occasional vagaries of the game and conditions. The integrity of the art, as the integrity of the game, depends on continuing to play by using the learned talent of forgetting about the bad shots. Each hole is a new opportunity to enjoy the skill that took years to develop into a high standard of play. Joy or devastation can be contained in each shot, and we don't know which will show up in our next lie. As a matter of experience and perspective, I am always hoping for joy. Each new lie, depending on your focus and ability, creates an opportunity to be joyful.

Golfers are optimists by nature. A pessimist on the tee or in any other position on the course is a *rarity*, in fact! If willing and properly trained, even a pessimist may even become an optimist on the tee, on the greens, and in the game.

## The Thirteenth Hole: Par Four, Blue Tee, 390 Yards

Secluded from the ocean view and the ferocious windstorm, the thirteenth tee was well protected from the elements. Running south to north, the fairway extends nearly four hundred yards to a slightly elevated, postage-size green. I have no memory of standing on the tee, but the drive ended in the center left fairway, in a spot exposed to all the wind and rain. The lie was setting up nicely. Intuition instructed me to put the driver on the ball and send it up close to the green. (My ego was humming out of control.)

The shot . . . the ball was skulked, and I didn't stay down on the shot. The ball rolled into the center fairway bunker, after which my driver came down into the turf like a sledgehammer, expressing the full force of my personal disgust!

The sheets of water were soaking the grass, so there was no way to address the lie with a descending swing. I knew that. So why use the driver? In golf, optimism is the patron saint but can also be a demonic temptress. Optimism thrives on honor and praise. What I had forgotten was that the weather needs to be respected and revered. I had forgotten the storm. A three-wood might likely have carried the ball into the garden spot. But my whole being was levitating in joy, so how could I think rationally? High on wind and rain and playing Pebble, it took a mere two more shots to land on the green—one out of the trap, the next right onto the green.

After a two-putt, I needed to collect my thoughts. I was staring at the Pacific Ocean, enjoying the power it was demonstrating. The surf was almost invisible, obscured by the heavy rain and turbulent wind. I stood there calming my mind and relaxing my wet, cold body—preparing for the fourteenth hole.

## The Fourteenth Hole: Par Five, Blue Tee, 572 Yards

More than a hundred yards to the dogleg, more than three hundred to the green. A wide open fairway inflated with wild wet air blowing inland *sans* impediment of any kind. From the tee, the landscape opens to a luscious vista, a panoramic view of several miles that takes everyone's breath away. Each of the four directions is like a fantasy. Imagine. To the west, the stormy ocean, covered with foam and filled with drama. To the north, the remarkable views of the semi-crescent majestic eighteenth fairway, where the surf splashes upon the rock wall that protects the exposed fairway and green. To the east, a half dozen established estates surrounded by large cypress trees overlooking the fourteenth fairway, the elevated sixth tee. To the south, basting in the rain, was Carmel in all its now rain-soaked glory. Its white beach lay naked of all living creatures. With enormous power the storm had taken control over the bay. Only one group of the nincompoop species was out. There we were! A dumb, brainless foursome. . . . Hard to believe! Just sloshing along the course . . .

My drive was wind-pushed into the near corner of the dog-leg, next to the rough. My second shot onto the elevated fairway wasn't much better. It landed in the rough along the right side. The marshal was in our wake again. Sherlock there was sort of stalking and observing us from the cart path on the left side of the fairway.

Freezing almost, we were all getting upset again. Finally, we were all on the sopping dance floor (the green), like Gene Kelly, just "dancin' in the rain"! With the wind at our backs, this should have been a breeze, but this gig was a storming tough hole to play. Although it was a stressful challenge that I had underestimated, it was still quite enjoyable.

*As in life as one moves along, experience teaches, using all the mistakes of the past. Quiet your mind, your body, and your voice, remembering those moments. Focus on the setup now; pause, seeing your target carefully . . . and then, with a full and purposeful swing, go through the ball with your right shoulder and finish your swing with your weight balanced on your left foot.*

The fourteenth green has a slight hill slope on the side running away from the pin, making it a *real bear* for putting—so, proceeding on, with tails well tucked, we walked off the green counting our blessed putts.

On the walk to the next tee, there is always time to reflect on the previous hole. In this case we didn't; instead, we stood tall and strode on to the fifteenth tee like war heroes. Determination and confidence were both required to address the storm and finish off this wild duel, not to mention keeping this deal we had made among ourselves.

## The Fifteenth Hole: Par Four, Blue Tee, 396 Yards

We appreciated the shelter available by the trees and estates on the left side.

The fifteenth fairway slopes gradually toward a swale next to the green. The right side of the fairway is lined with intermittent trees along the side of a roadway. My drive rested a couple of feet from one of those trees, with a clear shot to the pin. Face to the (howling) wind I came down on the shot with the three-wood; I pushed it toward the left edge of the fairway against the wind into the rough, just before the green. Chipped up below the pin, I two-putted this small green by which I had often stood in watch in past years.

Well . . . a "piece of cake" comes with courage, drive, fortitude, and love of the game. With personal pride, respect, knowledge and experience—that's how it all happens. Recovery takes place when fear of failing is confronting you. A little rain and wind do not carry the force that human determination releases when joy confronts regret. Deep within all golfers burns a fire that will not be extinguished by a little foul weather. It may be dampened, but the fire simply does not just whimper out!

*The drive is the opening curtain into the theater of personal joy, pain, and all the other emotional gymnastics experienced by golfers. Properly addressed, the driver will deliver a distance of great length, creating boundless joy and adrenaline rushes in a powerful golfer.*

*The drive has power to give sustenance; contrarily, it has power to discourage ownership of the very clubs, and bring on a desire to . . . well, sometimes, just to cry.*

*In the realm of golfing expertise, the drive carries the responsibility to fly that golf ball onto the garden spot on the fairway for the next shot. What brings this about, in sum, are so many factors—some known, some taught and learned through lessons, some experienced and learned through an osmotic, even mystical practice over time, and even through experiencing the obstacles and errors beyond which lies the miracle of expertise, gathered over a lifetime of play.*

In golf, as in all life, there can be a turning point during a round. That point had just arrived in playing the fifteenth hole. The fourteenth had been a downer, a real bear; it chewed me up and spat me out. So a "piece of cake" was in order on the fifteenth, then, to help me survive. And it was just that—it revived me, intact and raring to continue on.

In the last two minutes of most games, energy surges up and changes the complexion of the whole game. The last three holes in golf are the equivalent of those two minutes. They're the beginning of the increased amplitude in playing the best game possible. And that's a good thing, because the sixteenth, seventeenth, and eighteenth holes at Pebble Beach demand everything in the toolbox! And in the tank! Each one demands the utmost of respect as a longstanding theater staging world-class human drama; each is totally deserving of deepest honor and dignity.

We were almost as excited about arriving at the sixteenth tee as we had been at the first. The march through the course had been difficult, and we had survived the battle, shot by shot. Our confidence was rising to the occasion. Our character was holding up to the formidable challenge, as our attitudes were changing, becoming if possible even more positive about the play. We teed off with greater confidence, knowing we were gathering success swing by swing, chip by chip, and putt by putt.

Controlling my adrenalin flow into my muscles was my main concern, as I got more excited about the round. It was a lot more fun than expected. Cooperating, too, in building up the drama, the rain was even wetter and colder during the final holes we played.

## The Sixteenth Hole: Par Four, Blue Tee, 401 Yards

The fairway runs in a crescent configuration—surprising when you realize it. I didn't see the markers. My drive was straight, directly into the brunt of the storm and falling short into the rough. I recovered with a seven-iron to the slight dog-leg right. While rain and wind were bathing me with cold, wet air, I walked through the rough to the fairway.

My approach shot was an eight-iron pitch to the green across the open ditch. The pin was in the lower left corner. As I was putting out, I remembered that I had once touched Tom Watson on the shoulder at the exit to this green as he was leaving. His eyes were glazed in concentration as he pursued the trophy of the 1982 U.S. Open championship. "Hang in there, Tom," said I! To everyone's surprise, Tom's chip in from the rough at the seventeenth green won him the game at hand—by one stroke—over the star of this art, Jack Nicklaus.

On the green, I gladly two-putted the sixteenth.

## The Seventeenth Hole:
## Par Three, Blue Tee, 178 Yards

Viewing the seventeenth hole up close and personal was an exciting experience. The view was stunning, the storm careening into the picture I held from bright and sunny days of years past. There had been no letup whatsoever in the storm, projectiles of stinging rain aiming right into my face. In the distant mist, the flag on the seventeenth green was fluttering with exaggerated enthusiasm. We needed to drive a tee shot onto the green.

Well, I didn't reach the long narrow green with my drive—it was short, about thirty yards to the right of the fairway, in the wet rough. Baptized by the stormy gusts, a chip to the green was a blessing; two putts later, getting the ball in the hole was a gift of joy, honor, and humility.

*Scrambling in golf, just like serendipity in science, can be a real asset. When a shot has gone astray, then recovery has to be achieved. Recovery consists of the proper decision needed to compensate for a problematic shot. Knowledge, experience, presence of mind, and an ability to dig deep within are all necessary. Reaching down inside oneself in this situation brings out both integrity and confidence. Life flowing through you impels the very shots you need to pull out from the crashing dive into an emotional abyss. These precarious moments are absolutely necessary in learning this valued, and addictive, game of golf, just as in the game of life.*

Being humble, honoring the sacred ground we walk on . . . this is a part of golfing. As I gave thanks, that was the thought that came to me. Walking toward the eighteenth tee, I also realized that I hadn't lost a ball all day.

My mind froze in surprise at the information just received. It was true. Not one single ball!

A great deal of my awareness had been distracted, misplaced somewhere out there on the wonderful, beautiful course. My ball was always found, yet the distracted portion of my thinking hadn't been reined (rained?) in at all. My mind shouted aloud inside my noggin, "No! Oh, no! Cancel the thought!" But the worry was planted there. What was going to happen that I couldn't prevent?

I was on my way, the eighteenth tee in sight, and a touch of anxiety started to pulse through my senses. I walked up to the tee with reluctant gratitude.

It must be that the golfing gods exact the purest of homage by planting a fleeting thought in a golfer's head just seconds before the actual tee-off experience is completed . . . a warning of what is about to happen in the very next seconds . . . a premonition of an unalterable future. It is the eighteenth hole. Destiny has arrived! It has been set in motion, one's agreement isn't necessary—rather, this is a personal toll demanded by the gods to keep humility to the fore. Your reverential love for the game will give you the understanding needed to improve and sharpen your understanding.

Yes. The game is the teacher in all sports. A certain degree of brain freeze or mind fog is traded in exchange for some of the game's transformational power. Paying it forward for the specks of knowledge you are continuously receiving, even for each mistake you are enduring. Every round you play is a page in your file of knowledge. Playing with dignity, humility, and reverence is a primary principle, one of this game's teachings. Gratitude for its creation is a requirement, for this game gives more in return than any efforts it takes to play.

My cup of joy is filled with salt water!

## The Eighteenth Hole: Par Five, Blue Tee, 543 Yards

The layout of the eighteenth is something to behold. The tee alone has a stately presence. Its location has to be envied. Its grandeur has to be admired. Along with boulders, an extended stone seawall protects the fairway from the surf, for the full length of the 543-yard distance and ending beyond the green. On the opposing side, grand estates overlook the lush fairway, resting up there for decades.

In addressing the drive on the eighteenth tee, my thoughts were focused on the wind at my back. I had to put a perfect swing on the ball to take advantage of the wind. And it happened. The ball flew to the far side of the shallow dogleg, after which I planned to take the drive diagonally into the fairway leading to the green.

We all had good drives into the dogleg. I had stood next to that dogleg many times in past years, watching the pros play their second shot to the green. Now Jackie, Bill, John, and I were following in their footsteps.

I nailed my fairway shot with a three-wood—it sounded like a gunshot. The trajectory took flight straight toward the green. It was interrupted by a small branch, about the size of my index finger; the branch was growing on the tree in the center of the dogleg in the fairway. I never thought the tree would interfere with the flight of the ball. The velocity of the ball must have carried it into orbit. It was never found.

My earlier premonition on the walk to the final hole had come true. But the sense of disaster lasted only a moment. I dropped a provisional ball, and promptly drove it into the rough on the right side.

As we were walking down the fairway, we were liberating thirty years of withheld desire. The cloak of personal denial was melting away. My provisional ball was found. Then the next shot ended up in the bunker on the right side of the green.

With the final shot of our epic game nearly at hand, my thinking became personal. Having the idea to play Pebble and sharing it with my friends was the best idea in my repertoire of creative and miraculous events that year. I smiled and gave myself a pat on the back. I chipped out of the bunker.

In the end, we were all on the green, four friends drenched in joy and happiness, feeling gratitude seasoned with cold rain. We putted out. Game over. We had a group hug. A champagne lunch is being served in the dining room—shall we have a seat?

## Your Challenged Mind

To be philosophical: we receive our just rewards whenever serendipity happens. Having trust and faith in oneself and in the universe brings countless benefits, along with some fun surprises, in any human endeavor. On that day at Pebble Beach, we even received a trophy! The trophy we received was the souvenir of what has to have been the *greatest* golfing experience of my life. Playing golf in the freezing rain on my sixtieth birthday—wow, right on Pebble Beach—with my friends in tow was *absolutely awesome.* Four mature adults (using the term loosely) playing stormy golf, sheets of water bathing us with every shot. . . . People, we had the time of our lives, playing and practically drowning while walking into angry raindrops hurling into our faces.

Golf is not a hard game to play; it is *just plain difficult.* In life you have family and friends to lean on. In golf you have a chosen club and a ball with dimples all over it. The course condition, topography, landscaping, and weather are the physical elements of the challenge presented to you. Containing issues, your challenged mind, tormented by distraction and driven with an emotional transmission, are the internal machinery in play.

There are continuous challenges during the game of golf: calculating, examining the problem at hand, and prescribing a solution. Skillful eyes watching your application create pressure when you're trying to execute a shot. More experience creates confidence, which lessens the pressure while playing, while the learning curve of golf is continuous for years upon years.

No matter how severe or insignificant your golfing indiscretions are, they're written on the files in your memory banks for easy access. To shift your existing golf paradigm in a new, positive direction needs time, and plenty of mental and physical persuasion. Throughout a round, swings and shots are in constant flux and need corrective attention to be properly executed. This is true, of course, in any art, and the art of golf is no different in this respect.

Golf is a very personal game, to say the least. You need to recognize that playing the best game you know how is your best teacher. It will expose those apparent mechanical mistakes present in your address, mind-set, and intention. Before each swing, the slightest momentary errors are unnoticeable because blindly excited enthusiasm hides them, yet they become completely apparent after the club heads makes contact with the ball, resulting even at times in total disgust!

This can be experienced, as you progress around the greens, again and again, and yet again! How like life itself—and the old cliché of "practice makes perfect." In golfing, and playing the game, you can have fun while growing holistically into not only a better player—one with expertise in golf—but a better person, with some new experience in patience, acuity, and overcoming some lively challenges as well.

Taste every swing as a sip of fine wine from an awakened consciousness. But really, the feeling is sweeter than any wine. The bottle will always remain full as you taste the essence of this experience again and again. Executing your endeavors and feeling the experience with loving care—appreciating all this expanse of emotion, and its dynamic effects, with gratefulness—can give your life, in golf and in every other area of life, continued access to, as I have learned, some eighteen cups of joy.

As in life as well, playing golf carries a responsibility. This is as true for you as for those around you. Behavior has consequences and benefits. Proper etiquette includes disposition, manners, and courtesy, which are so valuable in playing any sport. They in turn give way to a friendlier rapport along with long-lasting respect within your foursome and other people with whom you play from time to time.

## The Game of Personal Discovery

Years of discovery, reading books and articles, practicing the sport as masterfully as possible, including some trial and error at the range and on other courses—even following lessons on the Golf Channel—it has taken me years to discover some secrets of the swing, along with secrets of the game and the art of synergistic golfing.

In the game of golf, as in all aspects of modern life, the magic of physics is a discovery in and of itself! The lever-releasing action of the club head producing acceleration right through the ball at impact is pure excitement. To be sure, directing that force into the ball requires total focus. Watching the ball be propelled through the air in the chosen direction is an exhilarating joy!

Some elements in golf take years to discover. Delicate, subtle, and invisible techniques become evident, as you realize how they apply within the course of play. Characteristics in my personality have adjusted quietly as I refined my own game while moving toward evolving into a bit of a more knowledgeable golf artist and more apt player.

Knowing that new abilities have been gained after years of striving has given me a wonderful sense of satisfaction. Passion, tenacity, perseverance with real grit, and just plain love of the game, all working together, have given me experiences that are thoroughly thrilling.

Scoring well is secondary to playing well. The art of this game is more about the dynamics, the synergy, the aspects of human vision, acuity, discipline, camaraderie, and the like . . . especially as the refining process continues.

Golfing entails, in every game, a path into the unknown, into a special space, a loop filled with anxiety, frustration, and discovery. The feeling is, at times, joy and freedom and an expansive happiness, exuberance, pure delight. This is a personal journey exploring the temperament, and courage, and a deep desire to dig into life and the sport, its obstacles and miracles, in pursuing a special worthiness as a player. This is about gaining expertise while having an active, experiential game going on. The game is authentically one of love.

## The Compass

Being grounded in a personal belief has amazing value in power and energy—a base from which to draw daily energy needed in life. This storehouse of knowing is available in all that you do and think during your day . . . even when the biggest of storms pour in.

Navigating the treacherous fairways of Pebble Beach Golf Links on my sixtieth birthday required having a rather precise compass, a compass contained within. At times, caught up in a difficult lie on the course, we humans forget to use this compass — with our minds so trapped by the rushing currents of anger, frustration, and distractions that focus and purpose and clear thinking seem nearly impossible.

Sometimes even our inner compass doesn't seem to be enough. There are times when even its directions are challenged. But holding to a course of action to the best of one's ability, come what may, brings all kinds of happiness into the game of golf, as much as in the experience of life. Extending little regard to the difficulty at hand, with the inner compass tracking all aspects of progress, there are no doubts about navigating such storms and obstacles . . . the weather, the intruding factors, or other apparent challenges to playing and enjoying a great and wonderful game fade into the colorful pleasures, and memories as treasures, in this art of playing golf.

## A Moment of a Lifetime

*Standing approximately ten feet away from a great surprise at the fourteenth tee has to be my favorite image from times past of that hole at Pebble. There he was. Tiger! Tiger himself! In person, right there!*

*His physical stature in addressing the drive off the fourteenth was demanding my attention. I waited there for a couple of hours while he began playing the back nine in the AT&T tournament. His swing was a flash, you could barely see the club head moving through the hitting zone. Lightning-fast. Wow. His swing balance was as smooth as cream. The ball wasn't seen coming off the tee heading toward the dogleg. It was a rifle shot.*

*Waiting for Tiger to tee off at the fourteenth was a blink of an eye in the realm of my personal reality. Having that memory for a lifetime is priceless. Time was a small price to pay for that personal gift from Tiger.*

*My reverence for Tiger goes way back. In 1995, I drove to Stanford to attend an intercollegiate tournament in which Tiger Woods was actually playing, with the sole intention of getting his autograph. He was nineteen years old. On the other hand, I was a fifty-five-year-old teenager. I had promised myself that, if Stanford hosted an intercollegiate tournament, I would attend. The tournament happened while Tiger was attending in just his sophomore year.*

*Walking the course, I asked the gallery members if they had seen him yet, as I was eagerly watching for him. A couple said he'd pulled a muscle in his shoulder getting out of the heavy rough. He was not playing on Sunday. My disappointment lasted only a moment. I was there and so continued to watch players from all over the country playing the front nine.*

*There were fantastic swings and excellent shots. By 11:00, at the elevated ninth green, I decided to head for home, disappointment aching in my heart. But my mantra is always to have trust and faith in the universe in all that I do and say, and successful outcomes will follow. You will see . . .*

*I bought a cup of coffee at the concession stand for composure. Walking down the steep grade toward the ninth tee, it seemed a group of spectators was forming on a raised knoll to watch the drive. Then, out of the corner of my eye, I caught a movement. Someone was coming towards me.*

*Unbelievable!*

*Tiger had been accompanied by a blond friend, and was now walking directly toward me. My heart was pounding in my chest cavity. He almost touched me as he and his buddy passed by. I gave thanks to the universe with my whole being while snapping out of a mild shock. A guy ran over and got Tiger's autograph.*

*As Tiger was signing my cap, I asked him, "How's that shoulder feeling?" With a full smile, he replied, "Hey. It's fine!" We shook hands and as he was walking away I said that he should eat and exercise! He turned, smiled, replied that he would, and said, "Thank you, sir!" "Good luck, and thank you," I replied. What an incredible surprise!*

*When I ponder that surprise now, it seems like a fully mesmerizing moment—to be in conversation with Tiger before he became Tiger Woods! Star golfer, the extreme professional golfer we know and love today—golfer extraordinaire!*

*Examples of magic . . . I am continually amazed how magic works in daily life. Not having stayed home to read the morning paper was a moment of magic. It was the best thing to do that morning. The universe works perfectly when the human species allows it do its thing without interruption and input, as in swinging the club without controlled resistance.*

*When you believe magic exists, it does. At times, in following intuition, numerous benefits appear rather out of the blue, all to enhance the enjoyment of life. In practicing this credo, I have become a happier camper. Abiding by the rules and principles the universe has to offer is a good thing.*

## The Triumph of Courage over Fear

Years ago, our foursome was playing a course in Yountville, a small village in the wine country of northern California. We were on the fourth hole. This fairway is 90 percent water up to the green.

I was first on the tee, with the wind blowing into my face at approximately twenty miles an hour. I couldn't believe what was happening to my knees—they were shaking. It had never happened before. My nerves were on edge, and I had to make a choice about which club to use. I chose my three-wood to play over what felt like 164 yards of white-capped ocean.

As I took my stance, my knees became turbulent. The swing had to be perfect to carry the ball over the expanse of water before me. Watching the ball flying over the water, to my surprise, it had found the grass a foot away from the pin, and then rolled past by about eighteen inches. Courage and trust were rewarded with surprised joy and gratitude. A downhill bird—eighteen inches away. It broke away at the lip. Reaching the pin was the gift I received for my turbulent knees on the tee.

"Are you going for the green?" I asked my brother John.

"No," he said, and he bailed out to the left. His ball was not found. Fear and lack of trust can also meet with pain and sorrow. Courage and fear are rewarded . . . equally in different currencies.

In golf, as it is in life, the universe provides a bag of tricks we need to understand and use so we can succeed in any endeavor. Moments of joy are given us when we face and confront adversity.

The game of golf, though it can bring on serious exasperation at worst, allows character to shine through—rain or shine—rewarding faith, trust, courage, and even the human being challenging the elements, taking risks, and reaching beyond where timidity might not always go. The game of golf is one in which all aspects of the mental, emotional, physical, and even philosophical person are called into action. It is an amazing dynamic—full of fun, learning, talent, and triumph.

A bird, a par, a double bogie,
A slice, a draw, a straight ball,
A drive, a putt, and all shots in between,
My swing and stroke have experienced all of these.

## The Connection

People, letting out the shaft, splitting the fairway, an iron to the green, dropping the putt—these are not what this game is about; they are only the legwork. This game is about enjoying laughter with warm conversation, creating endearing friendships that will endure over a lifetime . . . maturing relationships with respect for sportsmanship, which in turn bring joy into your life.

Popularity and golf have their reasons for being. They both have a purpose in bringing people together to play and converse.

In all seriousness, golf brings joy to many, sorrow to some, and an education to all. Golf was designed to bring out one's personal worthiness by trial and tribulation in touching on the internal force—the life force, the energy flow—the very soul of every golfer at heart.

The path to success is dotted with tests of worthiness. As each task is completed, the next one has greater demands, new circumstances to be confronted from a different position. A procedure has to be followed, which is demanding in structure. Physical ability, mental discipline, and spiritual beliefs all need to be exercised simultaneously.

Physical dexterity becomes challenged and is quickly exhausted, as is the emotional component of the challenge. Both levels of energy are fed by the individual's spiritual belief system, which is a constant. Physiological drain is evident. Respites are due as energies need replenishing.

The physical and emotional landscape becomes more attractive as you push on through a round. The hook of beauty and charm has been set to entice you to pursue the passion. The course is designed with treachery in mind so as to upset and interfere with your genteel adventure. Small tasks arrive on cue as your decision confronts the passion. As each demanding choice is made, the emotional and physical task is understood with a firm conviction, and at last the lesson is learned.

The inner voice gets sweeter as progress is reviewed and determined.

Understanding the complexities of golf demands instruction and continued practice with dedication. As golf becomes embedded in one's consciousness, the player's worthiness begins to shine through, sparkling at that.

Happiness enters into the belief system and big smiles begin. The art of playing golf is one of focus and fun, expertise in the artistry of the sport and the graciousness of approaching the game itself with honor and optimism—rain or shine—at all times. An amazing experience . . .

## A Cup of Joy

Friends, today we are gathered on
the first tee of this golf course.
We cannot forget the joy and laugher our
forefathers experienced on the
first tee of their golf course, their hearts filled
with enthusiasm, happiness, and dreams.
Now we are gathered to experience those
feelings within ourselves.
Our forefathers established the par, the birdie, the eagle,
and
The bogie on their own course.
They gave with loving hearts, devoted minds, so that
choosing to carry the club would
endure and never perish from this course.

We shall not exalt ourselves
before the first tee nor after the eighteenth green.
We shall again return with respect, dignity, and humility
toward properly addressing the ball.
Friends, we shall drink joy out of that cup.
For in truth, within ourselves the cup is filled.

# Appendix 1:
## The Art and Craft of the Swing

Known all over the world, golf has given joy, money, pain, and suffering to those who have swung a golf club. At twenty-four, I first held one in my hand, at Fort Benning, Georgia. Unaware I was a southpaw, I picked up a right-handed club and swung it backward. Nate, a friend, said, "You need a left-handed club." That was actually the beginning of a lifelong passion and foray, or adventure, into the wide (and wild) world of golf.

Being right-handed while playing left-handed has many disadvantages—frustration and fun, having to invert all the right-handed instructions. All the power seemed to be felt on my right side, along with coordination, dexterity, and natural strength to propel the ball off the tee. My right wrist has all the articulation necessary for bringing the club head speeding through the hitting zone. In my case, I need to use the left wrist to drive the club head through the hitting zone; but my left wrist has neither the articulation nor the dexterity, neither the coordination nor the capability to drive the club head through the zone. It took years of frustration at the driving range to figure out a solution for these dilemmas.

Swinging left began in my sports life when I was an adolescent playing baseball in a sandlot and city parks. I did it in imitation of Roger Maris, in fact. In the 1950s, Mickey Mantle and Roger Maris were left-handed baseball hitters, players all young fans wanted to emulate. Swinging like they did was a goal. . . . Now, I cannot swing right-handed with any coordination and power at all.

Having tried to work the left side as though it were my right side, it just wouldn't go! It won't do it! And years of quiet disappointment resulted. The solution finally came to me, years after watching Arnold Palmer swing: seeing how he moved his right side through the ball along with his shoulder, and examining his swing and body movement during the swing, it seemed he powered his exaggerated weight movement into the ball. His club-head speed was accelerated with that pronounced weight movement, creating a powerful centrifugal force through the ball with the right shoulder and body.

After applying that exaggerated movement to my left-handed swing for a number of weeks at the range, I became able to drive the ball farther. It has taken years of playing to gain confidence playing what is now my own way, and truly uniquely so.

As in boxing, giving the ball an uppercut at the tee guarantees that the club head is coming from inside to the outside of the swing plane. This swing plane will also give a draw when the face is a little closed. Pulling down and pushing the club head forward and low to the ground offers a square face to the ball that pushes it into the center of the fairway. This wisdom came to me out of the blue, simply intuitively, and I spent months developing it as part of my repertoire. The uppercut approach is a simple technique in swinging from inside out, as opposed to outside in with a right cross.

A right cross comes from outside in, with this swing plane creating a fade (if the face is square) or a slice (if the face is open).In both situations, the right shoulder must go through the ball beyond the hitting zone with velocity.

Another technique can be described using baseball imagery. For a right-hander, throwing the club toward first base will extend the swing plane. With this swing plane the golfer also draws the ball, creating forward roll for further distance. A left-hander needs to throw the club head to the shortstop to achieve the same results.

It took years of experimenting with the swing for me to understand the process involved in the complete golf swing plane and weight transfer. The elements of the golf swing are complex, and that is a major understatement. Personally, like many other sportspeople, I do not make any claims to understanding the physics of golf to any great degree.

While working with the swing at the driving range, I used to hit three small buckets of balls per week. I'd hit three balls with each club so I could feel the swing plane with that particular club and its normal distance when struck properly. The process of learning the elements with each club took about ten years. Applying those elements to each shot is the process I used to train myself to hit a certain type of shot with each swing. Knowing and using these elements is what makes golf both frustrating and fun—simultaneously—in this holistic dynamic of the amazing game's effects.

My left side isn't strong enough to drive naturally through
the hitting zone effectively. In making a shot, I have to con-
centrate on using the right swing for the club used for each
lie. Coming down on the shot is difficult for me, so, often I
sweep most of the shots off the fairway. The ball flight in turn
has a low trajectory, which creates a different mind-set in
playing iron shots to the green.

# Appendix 2:
# Understanding the Clubs

Woods, long irons, mid-irons, and short irons each have their own individual swing delivery through the hitting zone, all information that needs to be understood by any golfer. All golf strokes are a matter of power, touch, and feel. Power off the tee; touch and feel within a hundred yards of the green. Choosing the appropriate club for the shot you have to take will determine its success.

Woods are taken through the hitting zone with great club-head speed so that the ball will go the longest possible distance toward reaching the green. Similarly, the long iron controls a long hit toward the green. In windy and wet weather, a long iron, instead of a wood, is necessary for controlling the ball. Mid-irons are used for distance and accuracy in all types of weather. Short irons are used for accuracy and scoring. Because of the degree of loft in each iron, each one is chosen for a shot of a particular distance.

The putter is the most misunderstood club of all! At times it is the most dangerous, the most sensitive, the most hated, and the most loved club in the big golf bag. It is controlled by a sensitive touch that takes years of concentrated effort in practice, especially in developing an effective putting stroke.

*Do not allow the blue bird of paradise to stroke a
disturbing three putt on the velvet green of your mind.*
— my motto on the green

The pitching wedge, the lobe wedge, the sand wedge, and the putter are the instruments of touch and feel around the green.

The *feel* involves how you use the wedge to achieve the distance to reach the pin. This technique is developed with the understanding that the distance is short and that the swing force is under control. *Touch* is the sensitivity exhibited to control the energy of the stroke on the green. Touch takes several years and longer to develop. When achieved, it becomes a golfer's best friend in scoring.

Reading the slant slope of a green, commonly called the "break," is the key to putting. Most putts will involve a break to some degree. Touch is needed when putting, to control the roll of the ball along the break. Having a delicate touch with integrity is absolutely necessary in putting. It is impossible to hole out without it. In putting, patience has to take precedence over all emotions. The mind must stay quiet.

The structure of the putter is very important. Having the proper weight, balance, and feel is necessary if the player is to control the stroke. The sweet spot of the putter contains the innate static energy to drive the ball forward when putting. With a firm grip putting downslope, the toe of the putter is used. Its releases less active energy and controls the pendulum swing to roll the ball into "The Cup of Joy."

Thank you,
Christopher

# About the Author

Christopher Georgeovich has been a professional hair stylist and business owner for the past fifty years in the San Francisco Bay Area. When he is not working on his golf game, Christopher enjoys creative writing, photography and creating computer art in a style he calls "pixels-ism." He holds four design patents and is the creator of a "target golf game" that is to be played at golf driving ranges, as a way to improve one's skill at playing golf. Christopher's game, along with his other patented inventions are registered with US Patent Office. He is a forty year veteran, having proudly served in the United States Army.

# ABOOKS

ALIVE Book Publishing and ALIVE Publishing Group
are imprints of Advanced Publishing LLC,
3200 A Danville Blvd., Suite 204, Alamo, California 94507

Telephone: 925.837.7303  Fax: 925.837.6951
www.alivebookpublishing.com

CPSIA information can be obtained at www.ICGtesting.com
Printed in the USA
BVOW05s0534160714

358840BV00001B/6/P

9 781631 320064